# How to Read

# Your Bible

## Dr. George Guthrie

BiblicalTraining.org
Because Spiritual Growth Matters

How to Read your Bible

Copyright © 2018 BiblicalTraining.org

Requests for information should be addressed to:

BiblicalTraining.org
523 NE Everett St
Camas WA 98607

ISBN-13: 978-1987531800

ISBN-10: 1987531809

Printed in the United States of America

https://www.biblicaltraining.org/read-bible/george-guthrie

# Overview

Title: How to Read your Bible

Speaker: Dr. George Guthrie

## Goals

1. Be motivated to consistently read and study your Bible.

2. Get in the habit of observing the text of Scripture carefully so you understand the meaning accurately.

3. Learn how to use basic Bible study tools so you can understand the historical and literary context of a passage.

4. Learn the process of studying key words in a passage.

5. Get in the habit of praying that God will help you understand the meaning and application of the text.

6. What does the passage teach you about your relationship with God?

## Requirements

1. 9 sessions

2. 6 hours

## Prerequisites

None

## Format

Audio

# BiblicalTraining.org

BiblicalTraining.org is not-for-profit ministry that gives all people access to a world-class Christian education at no cost. Our classes range from new believers to biblical literacy ("Foundations"), deeper Bible study ("Academy"), and seminary-level training ("Institute").

We are a 501(c)3 not-for-profit and rely solely on the donations of our users. All donations are tax deductible according to the current US tax codes.

## DISTINCTIVES

**World class.** All Bible classes are taught by world-class professors from major seminaries.

**Holistic.** We want to see students move through content to deep reflection and application.

**Configurable.** Ministries can use BT lectures as well as their own to design their educational program.

**Accessible.** BiblicalTraining is a web-based ministry whose content is provided at no cost.

**Community-based.** We encourage people to learn together, in mentor/apprentice relationships.

**Broadly evangelical.** Our materials are broadly evangelical, governed by our Statement of Faith, and are not tied to any one church, denomination or tradition.

**Partners.** We provide the content and delivery mechanisms, and our partner organizations provide the community and mentoring.

# Table of Contents

# Your Speaker

Dr. George Guthrie is the Professor of New Testament at Regent College in Vancouver, British Columbia. As a student of the New Testament and Koine Greek, he is the author of numerous books and articles. Dr. Guthrie has participated in translation projects, such as the revision of The New Living Translation, and has served as a consultant on the Holman Christian Standard Bible, the New Century Version, and the English Standard Version.

George has also served for five years as a co-chair of the Biblical Greek Language and Linguistics Section of SBL, has served on the Executive Committee of the Institute for Biblical Research, and has served on the editorial board for Sheffield's JSNTS monograph series. At Union University he has led in the establishment of and serves as Senior Fellow in the Ryan Center for Biblical Studies, which is committed to promoting sound Bible reading, study, and interpretation at the grassroots level of the church. Dr. Guthrie holds both a Ph.D. and a M.Div. degrees from Southwestern Baptist Theological Seminary and a Th.M. from Trinity Evangelical Divinity School. For more information, visit his personal website at www.georgehguthrie.com.

## Education

PhD, Southwestern Baptist Theological Seminary

ThM, Trinity Evangelical Divinity School

MDiv, Southwestern Baptist Theological Seminary

BA, Union University

# Student's Guide

We are pleased that you have chosen to use materials from BiblicalTraining.org. We trust that you will find them to be of the highest quality and truly helpful in your own spiritual growth and that of your church. Please read through the following guidelines; they will help you make the best use of this guide.

## Weekly schedule

**Listen or watch the lesson.** The lesson for each chapter is designed to be listened to outside of your meeting. Each lesson lasts for an hour. This is a crucial step. If the meeting time with your fellow students is going to be productive and encouraging, everyone in the group needs to have listened to and wrestled with the lesson.

**Take notes.** This guide has the outline for each lesson with a summary of the teaching for each major point. If you are unable to take notes while listening to the lesson, please work through the guide at some point before your meeting.

**Questions.** Each chapter closes with a series of questions. Some of the questions are data based, confirming that you understand the information. Other questions are more reflective, helping you move beyond the important accumulation of knowledge to challenging you to think through what you are learning about God, yourself and others, and finally to application. Our encouragement is to think through your answers before your meeting and then use the meeting to share your thoughts and interact with others.

**Meeting.** Meet together with your group.

## Meeting Together

While some people may have to study on their own, we strongly recommend finding a group with which you can study.

A group provides encouragement to finish the class.

Interacting with others, their understanding and insight, is the most effective way to sharpen your own thoughts and beliefs.

Just as you will need the help of others from time to time, so also they will need your help.

# Mentor's Guide

If you are leading the group or mentoring an individual, here are some suggestions that should help you.

**Your role is to facilitate.** This is not an opportunity for you to teach. In fact, the less visible role you take, the better. Your role is to listen and bring out the best in the other people.

**Preparation.** Be sure to have done your homework thoroughly. Have listened to the lesson and think carefully through the questions. Have an answer for each question that will get the conversation going. A great question is, "What is the Lord teaching you this week?"

**Creativity.** What works to help one person understand may not help another. So listen to the conversation and pray that the Lord help you bring out the greatest interaction among all the people.

**Correct error.** This is difficult. If someone says something that isn't right, you don't want to come down on them, telling them they are wrong and shutting down their participation. On the other hand, if you let an obvious error pass, the rest of the group may think you agree and what was said was correct. So look for gracious ways to suggest that perhaps the person's comment was incorrect.

**Focus.** Stay focused on Jesus and the Bible, not on church or religious traditions.

**Lead the discussion.** People don't want to listen to a sharing of common ignorance. Lead by asking questions that will prompt others to think.

**Silence.** Don't be afraid of silence. It may mean nothing more than people are thinking. But if the conversation lags, then ask thought-provoking questions to get the discussion started, and then step out of the way.

**Discipleship**. Be acutely aware of how you can mentor the people in the group. Meet with them for coffee. Share some life with them. Jesus' Great Commission is to teach people to obey, and the only way this happens is in relationship.

**Different perspectives**. People process information and express themselves in different ways based on their background, previous experience, culture, religion and other factors. Encourage an atmosphere that allows people to share honestly and respectfully.

**Privacy**. All discussions are private, not to be shared outside the group unless otherwise specified.

**Goal**. The goal of this study is not just increased knowledge; it is transformation. Don't be content with people getting the "right" answers. The Pharisees got the "right" answer, and many of them never made it to heaven (Matt 5:20).

**Relationships**. Share everyone's name, email and phone number so people can communicate during the week and follow up on prayer requests. You may want to set up a way to share throughout the week using Slack or WhatsApp.

**Finish well**. Encourage the people to make the necessary commitment to do the work, think reflectively over the questions, and complete the class.

**Prayer**. Begin and end every meeting with prayer. Please don't do the quick "one-prayer-covers-all" approach. Manage the time so all of you can pray over what you have learned and with what you have been challenged. Pray regularly for each individual in the meeting.

# 1

## The Process of Reading your Bible

## Lesson Overview

The way you read and understand the bible affects the way you live. You make decisions based on your understanding of what you read in Scripture.

## CHALLENGES IN UNDERSTANDING AND APPLYING SCRIPTURES TO OUR LIVES

### 1. Cultural differences

The culture at the time and place the passage was written is different from the culture you live in.

### 2. Connecting what the apostle Paul said to our lives today

Each passage can teach you something about God and your relationship with him.

## A WORD PICTURE: BIBLE READING IS LIKE TAKING A TRIP

Bible study is like an expedition. You have a purpose in mind when you begin, the journey itself is an adventure, when you get there you discover things, and you bring back items and memories that are meaningful reminders.

### 1. We have to leave home

When you leave home, you are leaving a familiar cultural context.

## 2. The vehicle that gets us to our destination

Sound study process, good tools and right attitudes are what gets you to the destination of accurate biblical interpretation.

## 3. The foreign culture

Understanding the meaning of the text in its original context is a foundational part of the process of bible study.

## 4. The return home

What does the passage teach you about God and your relationship to him?

## 5. Bringing this all back home

How do you apply what you learned to your life today?

## CONCLUDING REMARKS

Read through Psalm 119 and write down as many benefits as you can that come from reading, studying and meditating on God's Word.

# Questions

1. How often do you read the Bible? What have you read this past week that has changed the way you think about God and your relationship with him? How did you apply it to a specific situation in your life?

2. How would you explain in your own words the metaphor that bible study is like taking a trip? Explain how one passage in the Bible that you read recently was an example of this process for you.

3. What did Dr. Guthrie mean regarding studying your Bible when he said, "If a text can mean anything, it doesn't mean anything? How does this make a difference in how you read and study your Bible?

4. What was the meaning of the passage in 1 Corinthians 8 to the people it was originally written to? What is the meaning of that passage to you and how should you apply it?

# 2

## Motivation for Reading your Bible

## Lesson Overview

Your motivation is a key to read and study your Bible consistently and meaningfully

## Review

Dr. Guthrie describes the process of studying the Bible by using the metaphor of taking a trip.

## BE MOTIVATED TO READ AND STUDY THE BIBLE CONSISTENTLY

You know that it will require some effort, but the reward is worth it.

## HINDRANCES TO READING AND STUDYING THE BIBLE CONSISTENTLY

### 1. Lack of discipline

You may lack the discipline to make interaction with the Bible a priority.

### 2. Lack of skills

If you haven't learned how to read or study the Bible, it can result in a frustrating experience.

### 3. Lack of motivation

If you lack the energy and initial desire to study the Bible, you might not begin the process.

## 4. Poor heart condition

If your relationship with the Lord is not good, you will likely find that you struggle to read or study your Bible. The parable of the sower is a word picture of different ways you can respond to God's Word.

## REASONS FOR READING AND STUDYING THE BIBLE CONSISTENTLY

## 1. It's a matter of obedience

God has given us a divine mandate to learn how to pursue him and love others by studying and meditating on his Word.

## 2. God's Word is a gift for life

The Bible teaches us how to live our lives in relationship to God.

### A. Through the Word, we know God

B.  Through the Word, we are blessed

C.  Through the Word, we have a positive impact on others

## PRACTICAL TIPS ON MOTIVATION

1.  **Be realistic**

    Set a goal that you are willing and able to accomplish consistently

2.  **Read and study the Bible in community**

    Reading and studying with others helps you to encourage each other.

### 3. Have a set time and place

Determining a set time and place helps you to make Bible study a pattern of your life.

### 4. Work hard at application

As your study of the Bible helps you to love God more and you change as a result, pray for wisdom to know how to apply what he's teaching you to your daily activities

### 5. Have the right tools and spiritual commitments

# Questions

1.  Rank the items listed as hindrances to Bible study in order from most impactful to least impactful in your life. Write a specific example for each one from your life. Then write one specific action you can take to begin overcoming that hindrance.

2.  Think of a time in your life where you have read and studied the Bible on a regular basis. What was motivating you at the time? What was your relationship with God like during that time? What caused you to discontinue that pattern? If you have never had that experience, what would you like it to look like?

3.  What would be the ideal routine in your current situation that you can imagine for reading and studying the Bible as a pattern in your life? What is one action you can take today to begin that process?

4.  As you obey God in reading and studying your Bible regularly, how does it affect your relationship with God? What is one thing you learned recently? How did it affect your relationship with God? How did it help you to love and serve someone better?

# 3

## Basic Tools for Reading your Bible

## Lesson Overview

Having and knowing how to use some basic tools for Bible Study can help you understand and interpret what you are reading.

### BASIC TOOLS AND COMMITMENTS NEEDED FOR BIBLE STUDY

### 1. PACKING FOR THE TRIP

You need the right tools and to know how to use them

## 2. Basic tools needed for sound bible reading and Bible study

### A. A good study Bible

Helpful features include a limited concordance, cross-referencing system, study notes, a subject index and maps

### B. Several translations of the Bible

General types of translations are formal equivalence, functional equivalence and paraphrase.

### C. Bible dictionary

Articles on specific subjects in the Bible can help you understand the cultural background.

### D. Exhaustive concordance

A resource that helps you do word studies

### E. Bible study software

Subscription websites with online resources provide helpful tools.

### F. Others

Personal mentors/study partners can help you process what God is teaching you.

## PERSONAL COMMITMENTS

### 1. Consider Your Pre-Understanding

When we come to the text and we think we already have all the answers, then we're not really studying to learn. We are studying to reaffirm what we already believe.

# Questions

1.  Read a passage like Ephesians 1 or Colossians 1 from three different types of translations. Begin with Formal equivalence (King James, New American Standard, ESV), then Functional equivalence (NIV, NLT), then Paraphrase (Living Bible, The Message). You can access each of these versions online at biblegateway.com. Type in the passage you want, choose the version from the dropdown menu, then click Search. Write out what God is teaching you as you read and reflect on each one. What words or ideas were interpreted for you in the paraphrase version? What advantage is there in using a formal or functional equivalence translation when you are doing a Bible study? In what ways was reading a paraphrase version helpful to you? How has reading different versions encouraged you to read the Bible more in a way that you can understand what it means and apply it to your life?

2.  Which of the basic Bible study tools do you have already? Which ones do you need to get? Have you investigated Bible study software programs like Accordance or Logos as a way of accessing these tools online?

# 4

## Background Studies

## Lesson Overview

Understand what the text says and set aside time to reflect on what the Spirit is teaching you. Knowing the historical and cultural background of the text will help you understand what it means

### PERSONAL COMMITMENTS (CONT.)

### 2. Rely on the Spirit

The Bible is a spiritual book that teaches you spiritual things so you need to rely on the Spirit for motivation, understanding what the text is teaching and when and how to apply the text you are studying.

3.  Be willing to submit to the text in obedience

    A.  You need to do exegetical work

        As we understand what the text says, our application
        should grow out of and be consistent with the
        meaning of the text.

    B.  You need to do devotional work

        It's important to apply the text to your own life before
        you try to tell someone else how to apply it to theirs.

    C.  You need to make heart space and life space

        Consciously determine to make your heart soft to
        receive what God is teaching you, and set aside time
        to read, study and reflect on the Bible.

    D.  Prepare to share your Bible study or reading

        Share what God is teaching you with a partner, a
        small group and people in your sphere of influence.

# BACKGROUND STUDIES

## 1. General historical background of the book

Answer the questions, who was the author, when was it written, why was it written and what are the concerns that form the backdrop of the book.

## 2. The immediate historical context of the passage

Understand the historical dynamics that affect the passage you are studying.

## 3. What cultural elements we need to study

Understand the cultural elements affecting the author and original audience of the passage.

# TOOLS FOR BACKGROUND STUDIES

## 1. Bible dictionary

Bible dictionaries have articles on a wide variety of biblical people, places and things.

## 2. Background commentary

Articles on background issues of specific books as they relate to the text.

## 3. Maps and atlases

Geography has a significant influence on the way people live and decisions they make.

## 4. The internet

You can search the web for resources on specific subjects. Verify the source to determine if the information on a specific website is accurate.

## BACKGROUND FALLACIES TO AVOID

## 1. Over-focusing on background details

Be careful that your study of history does not obscure the intention of the text.

## 2. Using outdated or misinformed tools

Confirm that your sources are accurate and reflect current information.

## 3. Ignoring the background

Keep in mind that the culture that the original audience was living in was different in some ways than the culture you live in today.

## HOW BACKGROUND STUDIES CAN HELP YOU

## 1. Background studies can explain elements that are not clear

Sometimes an important event or teaching in a passage makes more sense if you understand the historical or cultural background.

## 2. Background studies can help communicate the force of what is being communicated

Knowing the context in which a statement was made can help you understand why a statement was significant to people who originally heard it.

### 3. Background studies can help clarify application

If you understand how the original audience was expected to apply a passage of scripture, it can help you know how you should apply it.

# Questions

1. Pray on a regular basis that God will give you motivation and passion to read and study his Word. Do you notice a change in your attitude? Write down some specific ways you notice that the way you think and how you treat others is changing as a result of being motivated to read and study your Bible and applying what God is teaching you.

2. What does 1 Corinthians 2:9-13 describe the role of the Spirit to help us understand God's thoughts? Since the Bible was written to communicate God's thoughts to you, why is it important to rely on the Spirit to understand the Bible? Give an example of a passage in the Bible that the Holy Spirit has given you insight into its meaning. How has that changed your relationship to God? How has it helped you love and serve others better?

3. Give an example of a time the Spirit help you understand what a verse or passage meant. Give an example of a time the Spirit led you to share a particular verse with someone.

4. Give an example of a time that learning the historical or cultural background of a passage helped you understand it's meaning. How did it make a difference in how you applied it to your life?

5. What tools do you have to give you information on historical and cultural background? Which tools do you use on a regular basis? Which tools would be helpful for you to have in the future?

# 5

## Literary Context

## Lesson Overview

Context determines meaning. Understand the genre and literary context of the passage you are studying. Delete the Introduction heading and text.

### INTRODUCTION

Understanding the literary context of a passage helps you interpret it's meaning.

## MEANING IS FOUND IN CONTEXT

1. **Example 1: The phrase, "the danger of flying planes"**

   What this phrase means to you could be different depending on whether you are a pilot or a person on the ground watching an air show.

2. **Example 2: The word "table"**

   The range of meaning, depending on the context, could include a piece of furniture, a chart in a document, the level of ground water, or a verb (e.g., to "table" an issue in a discussion).

3. **Example 3: The word "stop"**

   When you are driving and approach a stop sign it has a specific meaning. When you are in an antique shop and see a stop sign hanging on the wall, you don't stop walking down the aisle because it's in a different context.

4. **Context shapes meaning**

   In order to understand what God is teaching you in his Word, you must pay attention to the context.

*How to Read your Bible*

## TWO MAIN AREAS

### 1. The broader literary context

#### A. Layers of literary context

Concentric circle diagram with passage, paragraph, section of the book, the whole book, Paul's letters, New Testament, the Bible.

#### B. Tools

##### 1) Commentaries

You can find a summary and an outline of the book.

##### 2) Study Bible

Most study Bibles will have an outline for each book.

### 3) Bible dictionary

> You will usually find brief article on each book of the Bible and an outline of the main points.

### 4) How to Read the Bible - Book by Book

> Suggestions about what's unique in the literature of each book of the Bible

## C. Example: Philippians 4:13

> Description of the meaning of this verse in its context

## 5. Biblical genres

## A. The rules of the game

> As you read different types of literature, there are different rules in play for understanding the intended meaning.

## B. Genres in the Bible

Genres in the Bible include history, personal letters, poetry and apocalyptic.

## C. Example: Psalms

The Psalms are a hymnbook that express worship to God. One type of Psalms is described as, "laments."

## D. Example: Proverbs

Proverbs Is a book of wisdom literature that was written to give you generalized truths about life.

## E. Example: The book of Revelation

A book of apocalyptic literature.

# HOW SENSITIVITY TO LITERARY CONTEXT CAN HELP US

## 1. Knowing the author's point

An author is usually trying to make a point using literary tools to build a message.

## 2. Adding to the Force of Communication

The context emphasizes the author's point.

## 3. Keeping application on track

The context helps us understand the message accurately so that our application can be consistent with the intended meaning.

# Questions

1.  What does "context" mean? Why is it important to understand the context of a passage of the Bible to determine its meaning? Give an example of a passage of the Bible where the context is important to understanding what it means to you and how you would apply it.

2.  What is the context of Philippians 4:13? What is the meaning of that verse to you? How would you apply that verse to your life this week?

3. What is the historical context of Psalm 18? How does knowing the context affect your interpretation of what it means? How does knowing the context affect how you will apply it to your life?

4. What are the main points that Proverbs 12:1-11 are teaching? How does understanding the context (i.e., Hebrew poetic literature) of this passage help you interpret the meaning accurately? How does understanding the context help you to know how to apply it to your life?

5. What type of literature is the book of Revelation in the New Testament? Why do we interpret descriptions like Revelation chapter 9 as symbolic? What is the intended meaning of Revelation 9? How would you apply that to your life?

6. In Numbers chapter 12, Aaron and his wife were critical of Moses because of the nationality of the woman he married? What was the nationality of the wife of Moses? When Miriam's skin turned white because of the leprosy, what was the visible contrast God was using to emphasize the seriousness of criticizing Moses as the leader God had chosen for the people of Israel?

# 6

## Observation

## Lesson Overview

Observation is an important skill in your daily life and also when you read and study the Bible.

### OBSERVATION: A KEY ASPECT OF BIBLE STUDY

Look carefully at the text because you cannot interpret or apply what you never see.

### MEANING OF OBSERVATION

Observation is doing a close reading of the text so that we notice, become familiar with, and hear the important details of the passage.

# HOW TO OBSERVE THE BACKBONE AS OPPOSED TO THE SUPPORT MATERIAL

The Backbone is the central idea. The support material helps you understand more about the central ideas in the passage.

## 1. The backbone

### A. Main verbs

Verbs give action to language.

### B. Connectors

Connectors that help you create a stream of thought are conjunctions, patterns of words and logic relationships.

## 2. Support material

Support material can include prepositions, personal pronouns, relative pronouns and adjectives.

### 3. Example: Psalm 1

Read and examine Psalm chapter 1 in a structured way.

## OBSERVATION: OTHER THINGS TO CONSIDER

### 1. Figures of speech

Metaphors and anthropomorphism are types of figures of speech.

### 2. Parallelism

Parallelism is when you make a statement and then repeat the statement in a different way to emphasize your point.

### 3. Key emotions

Enter into the emotion described in a passage of scripture.

*How to Read your Bible*

## CONCLUSION

Review Psalm 73, study Acts 1:8 by observing it carefully and thinking about it and study Mark chapter

# Questions

1. In the story describing when Samuel Scudder entered the classroom of Dr. Agassiz and thought his observation of the fish would be complete in 10 minutes, how long did he actually observe the fish? Choose something or someone that you see each day, observe them closely for a week and write down your observations.

2. What is the definition of observation that Dr. Guthrie gives at the 9 minute mark of the lecture? Choose a passage you have read or sermon you heard recently. Read/listen to it at least 3 times. What did you notice each time that you didn't see before? How did it help you understand more about your relationship with God? How will you apply it in your life this week?

3. How does Dr. Guthrie describe the parts of speech that make up the backbone of a passage? What parts of speech does Dr. Guthrie describe as support material? Read Ephesians 6:10-20, then look away and write out the main ideas in your own words. Then go back and separate out the verbs and write out the connecting phrases that go with each verb. Also note figures of speech, words that are repeated, etc. How does that help you understand the main ideas and the emotion with which Paul is writing this passage? How does that help you understand your relationship with God better? How will you live differently today as a result?

*How to Read your Bible*

# 7

## Word Studies

## Lesson Overview

Words have a range of meaning that depends on the context. Studying the meaning of key words can help you understand the meaning of a passage.

### TWO PRINCIPLES IN WORD STUDIES

### 1. Words have a range of meanings

Each word has a semantic range of meaning.

## 2. Context always determines meaning

The words, sentences and paragraphs surrounding a particular word help us to tune in to what that word means.

## ELEMENTS OF WORD STUDIES

## 1. Verbs

Verbs carry the action of a passage.

## 2. Key characters

There is often one or more key people that have an important role in a passage.

## 3. Repeated words

Sometimes you will notice a word or phrase that is repeated for emphasis in a passage.

*How to Read your Bible*

## 4. Difficult words

When you encounter a word that you don't know the meaning of, use a resource like a concordance, bible dictionary or bible study software to find the meaning.

## 5. Figures of speech

Find out what a figure of speech meant in the culture in which the passage was written.

## 6. Unclear, puzzling words

You will understand the passage better if you understand the meaning of each word in the passage.

## WORD STUDY FALLACIES

## 1. English-only fallacy

Sometimes it's difficult to translate the exact meaning from one language to another. Different English translations use different wording for some passages to try to convey the intended meaning.

## 2. Root fallacy

When a Greek word is a combination of two roots, the meaning isn't necessarily a combination of the meaning of the two roots. Two examples in English are pineapple and butterfly.

## 3. Time-frame fallacy

Applying a meaning to a word from a different era that the author was not familiar with when he wrote the passage.

## 4. Overload fallacy

Trying to apply all the possible meanings of the word instead of choosing the one that most closely fits the context.

## 5. Word-count fallacy

Interpreting the meaning of a word solely because it has a certain meaning a majority of the time, rather than determining what the context indicates.

# HOW TO DO A WORD STUDY

## 1. Identify key terms or concepts in a passage

Compare different translations for words or phrases they have in common in a passage.

## 2. Consult a concordance

Find other passages where the word or phrase appears and compare the context and meaning

## 3. Consult a good commentary

After you have studied, thought and prayed, consult a commentary to find out what someone else has learned in their study.

## CONCLUSION

Words have meaning, which has implications for how you interpret what the Bible says and how you apply it to your life.

# Questions

1.  What does Dr. Guthrie mean when he says that each word has a, "range of meaning." Give an example of a word having different meanings when used in two or more different contexts. In John 3:6-7, what is the difference in how the word, "born" is used (e.g., born of the flesh, born of the spirt, born again). How does this passage help you understand your relationship to God? How will you apply it in your life this week?

2.  In John 3:5, what do you think Jesus meant when he used the figure of speech, "born of water and the Spirit?" Look up this passage in a study bible and/or commentary. What are the possible meanings for this phrase? After reading John 3:1-15, what do you think it means? How does this figure of speech help you understand your relationship to God? How can you apply it practically in your current situation?

*How to Read your Bible*

3. In John chapter 3, what is the religious and cultural background of Nicodemus? Since Nicodemus thought that obeying the Law of Moses was the totality of living in relationship to God, what was Jesus trying to teach him by using the figure of speech of being, "born again?" What does this teach you about the importance of both being "born again," and also living a moral life consistent with what the Bible teaches? How does that affect how you will live today?

4. A Hebrew word that does not have an exact English equivalent is often translated, "steadfast love." It appears in Deuteronomy 5:10 and Psalms 26:3; 51:1; 86:13. Use a concordance or word study book to find more references where it appears. Using your reference materials, write out a definition in your own words. How does this help you understand God's love for you? How can you apply this today?

5.  Use a concordance or expository dictionary to find the meaning of the word, "sanctification." What is the meaning of the word? How does it help you understand the meaning of 1 Thessalonians 4:1-8? What do you learn from this passage about your relationship with the Lord? How will you apply it today?

6.  In Colossians 3, notice words/phrases that are repeated (e.g., put on/off, one another/each other). How do these words/phrases emphasize the main idea of this passage? What does this teach you about your relationship to God? How will you apply this today?

7. With a partner or group, choose a word/phrase/passage to study. As you are writing out your observations, choose one of the "word study fallacies" and write it into your text as if it is a legitimate observation. Share your word study with your partner or group, not telling them what you did, and see if they notice. How would this change the meaning of the passage? How would it make a difference in how you apply it?

# 8

## Application

## Lesson Overview

One of the most dynamic aspects of Bible study and Bible reading is when we see God transform us and it causes us to behave differently.

### PRINCIPLES OF APPLICATION

1. **Do the work of study and interpretation before application**

   Your goal is to hear the Word, be changed by it and respond to it.

*How to Read your Bible*

2. Get specific points of application from the passage being studied

   A. Write a summary of the original situation or problem addressed

      Accurately understanding the context is important to identifying the intended message of the passage.

   B. Write the general principles of the passage.

      Identify the principle in the text that is applicable to all people at all times.

   C. Apply the principle to specific current situations in your life that are similar to the original context.

      Be intentional about asking the Lord to help you apply the principle to a specific situation in your life.

   D. Example of possible application: Philippians 2:5-11

      Steps in interpreting and applying this passage.

### 3.  Apply to your own life first.

God wants to communicate personally to us through his Word in a way that affects how we live each day.

### 4.  Lead others to make specific application of the text to life

Communicate to others the meaning and principles in God's Word and encourage them seek the Lord on how they should apply it to their lives.

# Questions

1.  In the illustration about preparing a meal, what is the point that Dr. Guthrie is making about application of the Bible to your life? What is something you learned from a sermon you heard or a verse you read this week that you applied in a specific situation in your life? What is something you learned that you need to think about more deeply? How does it help you understand your relationship with God better? How can you apply it in your life this week?

2. Why is it important to do the work of study and interpretation first? What does Dr. Guthrie mean when he says to get the points of application from the passage itself to avoid, "springboarding?" What is an application in a passage that you have read in the past couple days? How can you apply it in your life today?

3. Why is it helpful to begin by writing a summary of the original situation or problem in a passage of scripture? How does this help you understand the meaning of 1 Corinthians 13? How does this help you to know how God wants you to apply 1 Corinthians 13 in the situations you face in your life right now?

4.  Go through these steps for Philippians 2:1-11. What is the original situation or problem? As you read and study the passage and pray about it, what is the Lord teaching you about the application in the passage? How can you apply it in your life in your current situation?

5.  Choose a passage you are reading and studying or a sermon you heard recently and go through the same steps in How does this process help you study, reflect and apply specific passages of scripture?

# 9

# Illustrate the Process

## Lesson Overview

Come alongside Dr. Guthrie as he illustrates the process of reading and studying your Bible by looking at the passage Colossians 2:6-15

### STEPS IN BIBLE STUDY

### 1. Choose the text and prepare spiritually

Prepare your heart so you are sensitive to what God wants to teach you.

2. **Study the backdrop**

   A. **Historical backdrop**

   It's helpful to know who the author is, who the recipients are and what the historical and cultural situation is.

   B. **Literary context**

   What is the context of this passage within Colossians and also in the Bible in general?

3. **Make observations on the central concepts, main verbal ideas and connectors.**

   A. **Central concepts**

   Read the passage in three different translations and write out what you think the main ideas are.

   B. **Main verbal ideas**

   Write out verbs that stand out and/or are repeated.

### C. Conjunctions

What are conjunctions that connect or contrast major ideas?

## 4. Do word study

Choose a word or idea that seems to be central to the passage and/or are translated differently in the different translations.

## 5. Write the general principles

Write out the main principle or two that the passage is teaching

## 6. Apply to similar situations in our context

Write out how this helps you understand your relationship to God and how it can be applied in general, and how you would apply it in your current situation.

## CONCLUDING REMARKS

It's helpful to read a passage using different translations. Translating the Bible from the language it was originally written in to English requires the translator to make choices about words and involves some level of interpretation. Languages are complex and English is constantly changing.

# Questions

1. Why should you pray before you read and study the Bible? How has it made a difference in how you notice and understand what God is teaching you in the passage? What does it teach you about your relationship to God? How has it made a difference in how you apply it in your life?

2. As you studied the historical backdrop and literary context of Colossians 2:6-15, what did you learn? How did it help you better understand the meaning of the passage? What does it teach you about your relationship to God? How will it make a difference in how you apply it in a current situation in your life?

3. What stood out to you when you observed the central concepts, main verbal ideas and conjunctions in the passage? How did it help you determine the meaning of the passage? What does it teach you about your relationship to God? How will it make a difference in how you apply it this week in your life?

4. What did you learn from one of the word studies? How did it help you better understand the meaning of the passage? What does it teach you about your relationship to God? How will you apply it in your life?

5. Choose a term in Colossians 2:6-15 and do a word study. Choose one of the "word study fallacies" and write it into your text as if it is a legitimate observation. Share your word study with your partner or group, not telling them what you did, and see if they notice. How would this change the meaning of the passage? How would it make a difference in how you apply it?

6. What are one or two principles that this passage teaches? What does it teach you about your relationship to God? How will you apply it to a specific situation in your life?

Made in the USA
Middletown, DE
06 November 2018